SAYINGS and PHRASES

Don't Look a Gift Horse in the Mouth!

(And Other Weird Sayings)

written by Cynthia Klingel ★ *illustrated by Mernie Gallagher-Cole*

ABOUT THE AUTHOR

As a high school English teacher and as an elementary teacher, Cynthia Klingel has shared her love of language with students. She has always been fascinated with idioms and figures of speech. Today Cynthia is a school district administrator in Minnesota. She has two daughters who also share her love of language through reading, writing, and talking!

ABOUT THE ILLUSTRATOR

Mernie Gallagher-Cole lives in Pennsylvania with her husband and two children. She uses sayings and phrases like the ones in this book every day. She has illustrated many children's books, including *Messy Molly* and *Día De Los Muertos* for The Child's World®.

The Child's World®

Published by The Child's World®
1980 Lookout Drive • Mankato, MN 56003-1705
800-599-READ • www.childsworld.com

ACKNOWLEDGMENTS
The Child's World®: Mary Berendes, Publishing Director

Katherine Stevenson: Editing

The Design Lab: Kathleen Petelinsek, Design; Victoria Stanley, Production Assistant

LIBRARY OF CONGRESS CATALOGING-IN-PUBLICATION DATA
Klingel, Cynthia Fitterer.
  Don't look a gift horse in the mouth! (and other weird sayings) / by Cynthia Klingel.
      p. cm. — (Sayings and phrases)
  ISBN 978-1-60253-206-9 (library bound : alk. paper)
  1. English language—Idioms—Juvenile literature.
  2. Figures of speech—Juvenile literature. I. Title. II. Series.
  PE1460.K6835 2009
  428.1—dc22   2009001639

Printed in the United States of America
Mankato, Minnesota
May, 2010
PA02063

People use idioms (ID-ee-umz) every day. These are sayings and phrases with meanings that are different from the actual words. Some idioms seem silly. Many of them don't make much sense . . . at first.

This book will help you understand some of the most common idioms. It will tell you how you might hear a saying or phrase. It will tell you what the saying really means. All of these sayings and short phrases—even the silly ones—are an important part of our language!

TABLE *of* CONTENTS

Achilles' heel

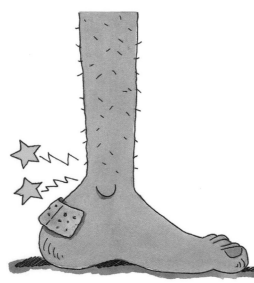

The baseball game between the Eagles and the Panthers was in the ninth inning. The Eagles were one run ahead, but the Panthers' best hitter was
up to bat. Mike, the Eagles' pitcher, was nervous. His coach walked out to the mound.

"I saw this kid play last week," the coach said. "Throw him a curveball—that's his Achilles' heel."

MEANING: A person's area of weakness. In Greek mythology, Achilles' mother dipped him in the River Styx to protect him from harm—but she held him by his heel, leaving that part unprotected.

Brownie points

Molly didn't like cleaning, but she'd been working on her room for hours. Now it was spotless. She was making her bed when she heard her mom come home.

"Hey Mom, I have a surprise for you!" she called out.

"Wow, this is great," said Mom when she saw the room. "You've really earned some brownie points today!"

MEANING: To get credit for doing something that makes someone else happy or that someone appreciates

Busy as a bee

Hannah's grandmother was a great gardener, and Hannah loved helping her. Hannah learned how to hoe and weed, and she had fun picking strawberries and green beans.

"Grandma, I'm going inside to get a drink. Do you want something?" asked Hannah.

"I'd love some lemonade," replied Grandma. "We'll sit together and rest. You've been as busy as a bee!"

MEANING: To be very busy getting things done

The chips are down

Jamie and his dad were watching their hometown football team try to win a close game. The coach had called a time out and was talking to the players.

"There's only time for one more play," said Jamie. "Do you think they can score?"

"Keep an eye on Burnside, the wide receiver," said Dad. "When the chips are down, he's the best choice. Nobody does better under pressure."

MEANING: When someone is in a desperate situation; when someone has one last chance to make something work

Cut-and-dried

The citywide talent show was coming up, and Sara had ideas for some changes. "They'd make the show more interesting," she told her mom.

"Those are great ideas," said Mom, "but I don't think the committee will want to make changes this late. They've been doing this event the same way for years. Everything is pretty much cut-and-dried."

MEANING: Prepared ahead of time; not subject to change

Don't look a gift horse in the mouth

Katie's aunt had just bought a new computer and given Katie her old one.

"It works OK," said Katie, "but it's not as nice as the one I wanted."

"It's not quite as fast," Dad agreed, "but it's still pretty nice, and it didn't cost us a cent. Don't look a gift horse in the mouth!"

MEANING: To accept and appreciate a gift, even if you're not sure about it

To: YOU

Dropping like flies

The dance finals were tomorrow, but things weren't looking good for Grace's team. The flu was going around, and Grace had been sick for two days. The phone rang, and a few minutes later, Grace's sister walked into the room.

"Bad news," she said. "Ms. Wilkins says the girls on the team are dropping like flies! Three more of them have gotten sick."

MEANING: When a number of people leave or drop out from an activity

Elbow grease

Nikki's parents were looking for a new house. One day, they came home really excited.

"We found it!" Mom said. "It's a great place. Come on, and we'll show you."

"Eeewww," said Nikki when she walked inside. "Didn't these people ever clean?"

"It's pretty dirty," Dad agreed. "But we can take care of that with a little elbow grease. Come look at this great backyard!"

MEANING: Hard physical work

A fish out of water

"What a day!" Mom sighed as she put down her bag.

"What happened?" asked Nate.

"I helped teach some programs for first-graders," answered Mom. "I'm exhausted!"

"Why? You're used to teaching," Nate asked.

"I'm used to teaching high-school students!" Mom replied. "I haven't taught first grade for years. I really felt like a fish out of water."

MEANING: Doing something that you aren't used to doing (or that you haven't done before); feeling uncomfortable or as if you don't belong

Fit as a fiddle

Keneesha was excited. Grandpa was visiting today, and she hadn't seen him for weeks. He'd been in the hospital, and Keneesha had been worried about him.

"Keneesha!" exclaimed Grandpa as he gave her a big hug.

"Hi, Grandpa!" replied Keneesha. "It's great to see you. I was really worried!

"No need to worry about me," said Grandpa. "I'm fit as a fiddle!"

MEANING: Healthy or in good shape

A fly on the wall

Brittany was causing problems on the soccer team. She was bossy and rude, and she didn't want to practice.

"I heard the coach is going to give her a warning," said Emmy. "Behave—or be off the team!"

"Wouldn't you love to be a fly on the wall during that meeting?" said Jenna. "I'd love to hear what the coach says to her."

MEANING: Wanting to know what is happening or being said when you are not present

Hook, line, and sinker

Toby and Brianna were planning a surprise dinner for their mom's birthday. They needed to get Mom out of the house while they cooked. Dad offered to help.

"I told her I need help picking out a present for Grandma," he said.

"Did she fall for it?" asked Brianna.

"Yup—hook, line, and sinker!" said Dad. "Now, get busy! We'll be back here by six o'clock."

MEANING: To believe something completely; to be completely taken in by something

In your face

It was the beginning of basketball season, and Chris was playing center for the first time. The center on the other team played hard, pushing against Chris and fouling him twice.

"Chris," said the coach afterward, "you did a great job. That kid was really in your face, but you didn't let it bother you."

MEANING: When someone is being aggressive and annoying you

Lend an ear

Something was bothering Shania. She wasn't saying much, and she seemed unhappy.

"Is something wrong?" asked Rosa. "You seem awfully quiet."

"No, I'm okay," said Shania. She looked down and sighed. "I guess it's nothing important."

"Well," said Rosa, "if you want to talk about it, just let me know. I'm always ready to lend an ear."

MEANING: To be a good listener, especially when someone needs to talk about a problem

Loose cannon

The football season was starting up, and Todd and Zeke were big Hawks fans.

"Who do you think they're going to start as quarterback?" asked Todd.

"Martinez," said Zeke firmly. "He's so reliable."

"How about Dunn?" said Todd. "He's got an amazing arm."

"Yes," Zeke replied, "but you never know what he's going to do. He's kind of a loose cannon."

MEANING: Someone who is unpredictable or acts in unexpected ways

Mind over matter

Kelly's room was a mess, and Mom said she couldn't go to the movie that night unless it was clean. Kelly looked around at all the clothes and games and toys.

"I'll never get this done in time!" she cried.

"Sure you will," said Mom. "Mind over matter! Tell yourself you can do it, and you'll get it done."

MEANING: A way to convince yourself that you can do something

My hands are tied

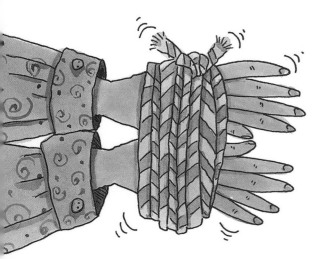

Annie and Jared were in charge of ordering t-shirts for the drama club, and they were trying to change the design.

"Jared came up with this new idea yesterday," Annie said to Mr. Larsen. "We really like it! Can't we use it instead?"

"Sorry, Annie," said Mr. Larsen, "but we turned in the order Monday. It's too late to change it. My hands are tied!"

MEANING: When you can't change something or make a different decision, even if you want to; not having any choice

Nothing to sneeze at

Luke thought today's baseball game had gone pretty well. He had gotten to pitch for three innings. He'd struck out three batters, and no runs had scored.

"Good job!" said Luke's older brother, Alex.

"Yeah, but I only played three innings," complained Luke.

"Hey," said Alex, "three innings, three strikeouts, and no runs—that's nothing to sneeze at!"

MEANING: Something that shouldn't be ignored; something that is good or important

Opening a can of worms

Tyler was working on a group science project.

"How did your meeting go?" asked his mom.

"Not very well," Tyler replied. "We can't agree on how to get this thing done. Today we started talking about choosing another project."

"Oh, boy," said Mom. "That would really be opening a can of worms. You had enough trouble deciding on this one!"

MEANING: Starting something that could lead to trouble or problems

Over the hill

The house was decorated with balloons and streamers, and the cake was on the table. Everything was ready for Dad's surprise party. It was his fortieth birthday!

"Surprise!" everyone yelled as Dad walked in the door. A smile stretched across Dad's face. Mom walked over and gave him a hug.

"How does it feel to be over the hill?" she asked with a wink.

MEANING: To be old; often used when people turn 40

Pecking order

Joey had just started his first job, stocking shelves at the grocery store.

"How did it go?" asked Dad.

"It was confusing," Joe replied. "Everybody was telling me what to do. The manager, the cashiers—even the other stockers! I didn't know who to listen to."

"Right now you're the new guy," explained Dad. "Pretty soon you'll know where you are in the pecking order."

MEANING: The order of power in a group of people—who can give orders to whom

PECK PECK

PECK PECK

PECK PECK

PECK PECK

PECK PECK

Pull some strings

Maria was excited! Her favorite singer was going to give a concert in Maria's town. She ran home to ask her parents if she could go.

"I'm sorry, Maria," said Dad. "I heard the tickets are already sold out. But I have a friend who works at the radio station. May he can pull some strings and find us tickets."

MEANING: To use connections or influence behind the scenes to get something done

Put a sock in it

Robbie's family was on a long road trip, and five-year-old Micah was unhappy.

"This is boring!" he kept saying. "I want to go home."

"Oh, Micah, put a sock in it!" Robbie pleaded. "You're being really annoying."

"You know," said Mom with a laugh. "I remember somebody else who used to complain on long trips, when he was little."

MEANING: Said to someone to get them to stop talking or complaining

Rain or shine

Claire was helping set out food for the family's backyard party. But dark clouds were gathering in the distance.

"What will we do if it rains?" she asked. "Will we have to cancel the party?"

"Oh, no," answered Mom. "There are lots of people coming, and there's a lot of food to eat! This party will go on, rain or shine!"

MEANING: No matter what the weather is like

Rub someone the wrong way

Matthew and his buddies were going to the park to play some basketball.

"Did you ask Jason if he wanted to play?" one of them asked.

"No, I didn't," answered Matthew. "He's not a bad guy, but I don't really like being around him. I'm not sure why, but he rubs me the wrong way."

MEANING: To be annoying to someone

A stick in the mud

"I don't want to go on a boat ride!" said Ben.

"Ben," sighed his sister Anna. "It's our last day at the lake. Everyone wants to have fun. But you don't want to swim. You don't want to go on a boat ride. You don't want to do anything. You're just being a stick in the mud!"

MEANING: A person who doesn't want to do fun things

Talk turkey

GOBBLE GOBBLE GOBBLE

The first quarter was almost over, and Kyle was having some trouble. His teacher, Mrs. Green, was doing her best to help him.

"All right, Kyle," said Mrs. Green. "Let's talk turkey. You're doing really well in your other subjects, but you're way behind in math. What do we need to do to get you caught up?"

MEANING: To discuss something serious or important; to have an important conversation

Tongue-in-cheek

Zachary was growing fast, and he was hungry all the time.

"Would you like a ham sandwich?" his mom asked.

"I don't know," said Zachary. "Dad said that if I keep eating this much, he'll start taking grocery money out of my allowance!"

"Oh, he wasn't serious, silly!" said Mom with a laugh. "He was just speaking tongue-in-cheek."

MEANING: Used to describe something said in a joking or teasing way

Walking on eggshells

Emily's older sister was nervous about choosing a college, and she was getting cranky with her family.

"Don't let it bother you," Mom said to Emily. "You know she's not usually like this. She'll feel better when she makes her decision."

"I know," said Emily, "but it's hard to be around her! I'm always afraid of saying the wrong thing. It's like walking on eggshells!"

MEANING: Being careful not to annoy someone; being on your best behavior

UH-OH

The whole kit and caboodle

The school carnival had lots of fun games, contests, and prizes. Finally it was time for the grand-prize drawing.

"The winner…," said Mr. Olson, "is Tanner Simms!"

Tanner ran to claim his prize. On the table was a huge basket with toys and treats.

"Which ones did I win?" he asked.

"It's all yours!" replied Mr. Olson. "The whole kit and caboodle!"

MEANING: Everything

You can't teach an old dog new tricks

Kelsey had been helping Grandma learn how to use her computer. This time, Kelsey was trying to teach her how to open photos she received by e-mail.

"You click here," said Kelsey, "and then there."

"Oh, Kelsey," sighed Grandma. "Sometimes I think I'll never figure this out. You know, you can't teach an old dog new tricks! Thanks for being so patient."

MEANING: Learning a new approach can be hard, especially if you've been doing something one way for a long time.